AF428667

Dedicated to
my mother (Zera), my son (Austin), my goddaughter (Ella)
my darling loves Arenike & Irede
and
my husband (Wendell)
for encouraging me to follow my dreams.

Loving you back to
my siblings: Aaron (RIP), Phia, Kindel (RIP), and Jessica
my cousins; Nikki, Debra, and Frank

Email@marymartingordon@gmail.com
ISBN: 979-8-218-95578-6

Gorenflo Elementary
Have a good day at school my dear.
I will Mom!
Hmmm, I am going to make at least one new friend today.
Oh Zera, I just love your positive attitude!

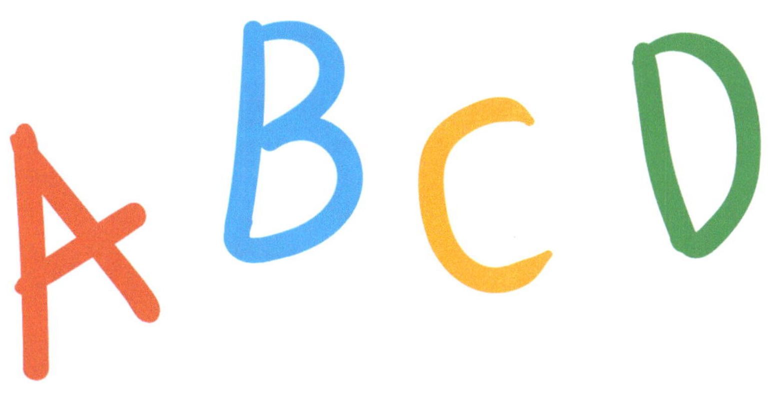

Good Morning!
My name is Ms. Hunt.
Please stand up when I call your name
and tell us three things that you like.
Let's go in alphabetical order.

My name is Austin.

I like ants, apples, and airplanes.

My name is Brian.
I like bees, beans, and balls.

My name is Carmen.
I like coins, cards, and cats.

My name is Debra.
I like dogs, dolls, and drums.

My name is Ella.
I like earth, eggs, and elephants.
E
e

My name is Frank.
I like fans, foxes and fish.

My name is Getta.
I like gifts, gum, and giraffes.

My name is Hannah.
I like hearts, hats, and home.

My name is Ian.
I like ice cream, insects, and igloos.

My name is Jessica.
I like jam, jokes, and jump ropes.

My name is **K**indel.
I like **k**iwi, **k**ites, and **k**ebabs.

My name is Luca.
I like Lizards, Lions, and Lemons.

My name is **Martin**.
I like **m**usic, **m**angoes, and my **m**om.

My name is Nikki.
I like nuts, nets, and naps.

My name is Onan.
I like oak trees, oranges, and owls.

My name is Phia.
I like playgrounds, pools, and pizza.

My name is Quimby.
I like quarters, quills, and quiet.

My name is Rede.
I like roses, rubix cubes, and rainbows.

My name is Sage.
I like seahorses, sand, and salads.

My name is Tony.
I like trains, trees, and tacos.

My name is Umaria.
I like umbrellas, ukuleles, and unicorns.

My name is Verna.
I like **v**egetables, **v**ests, and **v**iolins.

My name is Wendell.
I like whistles, watches and water.

My name is Xander.
I like x-rays, ximenas, and xylophones.

My name is Yuma.
I like yo-yos, yams, and the color yellow.

Hmmmmp...why am I always last?
I know, "Z" is the last letter in the alphabet
and my name starts with the letter "Z".
My name is Zera.
I like zebras, zippers, and zoos.

Well done students!
Meet your new friends,

Friend from A to Z

I did it Mom! I made at least one new friend!
I made a bunch of new friends!
Mom: I knew you could do it. Who loves you?
Zera: You!
Mom: Yay!!!
Mom: Who loves me?
Zera: Me!
Mom: Yay!!!
AM
KG
ZG
PW
MMW
JG

Write three things that you like

1 _______________

2 _______________

3 _______________

The Adventures of Zera series
is dedicated to my mother,
Zera B. Gordon.
She showed me
the meaning of a Mother's Love
and Austin and I
are forever grateful.